How to Conduct Successful Employee Opinion Surveys

A Survey Administration Manual

by
Louis E. Tagliaferri, Ph.D.

Published by
Talico Developmental Systems L.C.
4304 Blue Heron Dr.
Ponte Vedra Beach, FL 32082
904-285-7757
www.talico.com

Contents

Preface

The manual introduces executives, managers and human resource professionals to a process by which they can conduct a successful employee opinion survey in their organization. The focus of the manual is on planning, execution and follow-up, three key elements that are requisites for a successful employee opinion survey project. Readers will find that the manual contains a wealth of valuable information including a step-by-step survey planning guide, model project schedules, sample survey announcements to employees, examples of survey reports with interpretation guidelines and a recommended process for post-survey follow up response action. All of this information is presented in a way that will be easily understood and that can be easily applied or administered by any management level employee.

All members of management who may function as their organization's survey project team to read this manual in its entirety before launching any survey activities. Managers and supervisors who may later be assigned responsibility for interpreting survey results and for developing appropriate response action will also benefit from reading relevant sections of the manual during the course of the survey project.

There is one final comment about the purpose and utility of this manual. Not only is it an excellent guide for those who are planning to conduct an employee opinion survey in their organization, but also it is an important component of the employee opinion survey services that are provided by Talico Developmental Systems L.C. (Talico). All Talico survey clients are provided with a copy of this manual as a first step in their survey planning process. Throughout the manual the reader will find, therefore, reference to various aspects of the "Talico Survey Process."

Introduction

The global economic slowdowns of the years 2008 through 2010 have focused the attention of senior management in all sectors of business and government even more closely on the effective utilization of an organization's most valuable assets, its human resources. Before the beginning of this century there were great advances in production systems, technology, a voracious market appetite for new consumer and industrial products and the ability to pass along price increases for material, labor, energy, capital and other costs of production to customers. These factors enabled organizations to achieve nonlinear increases in earnings. But, the recessionary global economy has severely restricted that method of attaining corporate profitability and it is likely that for the foreseeable future profit growth for most organizations will be a function of increases in labor productivity. An important attribute of effective human resources utilization is management's willingness to listen and respond to employees' interests, needs, concerns and suggestions. One of the best ways to accomplish this is for an organization to conduct an employee opinion survey, a process for diagnosing organizational conditions that traces its history to the pre-World War II era.

Before the 1940s the concept of scientific management assumed that employees readily accepted their traditionally prescribed roles. Job tasks were simplified through fragmentation so that they could be easily performed by the average worker who at the time was unskilled and poorly educated. Jobs were highly structured, leaving little room for a worker to exercise independent judgment. Increases in labor productivity were achieved through industrial engineering techniques, technological advances and by motivating workers using the principle of reward and punishment. Because it was assumed that individual workers had little to contribute in terms of creativity or innovation management believed that no useful purpose would be served by listening to employees' ideas or suggestions. Moreover, because of the practice of benevolent autocracy that was prevalent during that time management was convinced that it knew what was best for employees and therefore there was neither a reason to pay much attention to any interests, needs and concerns that they might express.

This changed dramatically when productivity became a major concern during World War II. In response to productivity concerns on the part of the military-industrial complex Rensis Likert and Elmo Wilson conducted several important studies to determine the relationship of morale and motivation to absenteeism and productivity. In order to obtain the information they needed for their studies the two researchers developed data collection instruments that became the forerunners of today's employee opinion surveys.

In 1946 Likert and his colleagues formed the Survey Research Center at the University of Michigan. They used surveys to gather data and information about many different aspects of the culture of organizations. One major result of these efforts was the development of the concept of organizational psychology which differs from industrial psychology which focuses on the collective behavior of employees in organizational systems and subsystems rather than on the behavior of individuals within those systems. Today, employee opinion surveys are the most common method for obtaining diagnostic information about conditions that can affect labor productivity. The information that is obtained from these surveys is used by organizational development professionals to assist management in their efforts to improve the effectiveness of organizational subsystems such as communication systems, human resource utilization, and performance management systems including cost reduction and quality improvement, inter and intra-work unit relationships (team building) and much more.

Employee opinion surveys can identify human factor related issues that may be unknown to management, provide clarity about known issues, and even localize issues to specific demographic subgroups of employees. They can provide management with an insight into the reasons for the behavior and perceptions of employees and obtain invaluable feedback and information from employees about ways by which work operations can be made more effective and efficient. Because of this it is not surprising that the majority of leading organizations use periodic surveys to assess the attitudes and opinions of their employees.

The Organization Climate

Daniel Katz and Robert Kahn define *organization climate* as the collective norms and values of an organization's socio-technical systems. In addition, they suggest that organization climate reflects "the history of internal and external struggles, the types of people the organization attracts, its work processes and physical layout, the modes of communication, and the exercise of authority within the system." According to this definition, an organization climate covers many objects within an organization's subculture, ranging from organization policy, leadership and the way that management communicates with employees, treats them and uses their skills to work methods, physical work conditions and other work environment issues. An employee opinion survey is a measurement instrument, usually consisting of a series of structured questions or statements that evaluate employees' perceptions about the various objects and attributes that together comprise the organization climate. This type of survey is also known by several other names, including but not limited to *organization climate survey.*

The term "organization climate survey" is actually generic to a class of measurement instruments that are used to the various attitudinal objects and attributes that are referenced above. As the field of organization development grew the number of researchers in the field proliferated, as did the number and type of diagnostic instruments that were used to measure organization climate characteristics. Because of this since Likert began using his *Survey of Organizations* questionnaire, a number of other terms have become synonymous with the term *organization climate survey. Employee Opinion Surveys, Employee Attitude Surveys, Work Climate Surveys, Surveys of Organizational Characteristics, Job Satisfaction Surveys, Employee Morale and Motivation Surveys* and many other names and titles today characterize the type of survey instrument that measures, in one form or another, objects and attributes of an organization's climate, as defined earlier.

For purposes of illustration, the survey process presented in this manual focuses on an *Employee Opinion Survey* developed by Talico Developmental Systems L.C. which is designed to measure a broad spectrum of organizational characteristics. Others types of surveys are more object specific. For example, the Talico *Communication Effectiveness Scale* focuses only on various attributes of managerial communication within organizations. Its purpose is to give managers and supervisors feedback about how others within the organization perceive their communication skills. Similarly, the Talico *Management Practices Inventory II* is an organization climate survey that evaluates key managerial and leadership work behaviors.

One very important characteristic that all organization climate surveys share in common is that they measure perceptions – not necessarily fact. Organization climate surveys provide a metric for the way employees perceive work environment conditions, how they "feel" about various work related situations that may affect them, and what they think or believe about the organization in which they are employed, their supervisors, senior management and even about their coworkers. But, when survey data are studied the reader or analyst must remember that he or she is reviewing data about perceptions. For example, an organization climate survey might find that 65% of the employees surveyed believe that most of the better jobs within their organization are filled by management hiring new people from outside the organization. That is perception, not necessarily fact.

The only way to determine whether perception is also fact is for the organization to review its documented records that show how many vacancies existed over a certain period of time, how many were filled and whether the vacancies were filled through internal promotion (or at least a job bidding procedure) or by hiring new employees from outside the organization. Still, it must be clearly understood by management that a perceived work related problem or inequity can have the same negative affect on morale and productivity as a problem or inequity in fact. A challenge for any management that conducts an organization climate survey is to separate perceived problems from factual problems and then correct both to the extent possible.

The knowledge, skill and expertise of the organization climate survey scale designer together with the use of recognized scale construction procedures are employed in the development of a valid and reliable survey instrument. Because survey design and development are complex processes, they should never be attempted by inexperienced or untrained personnel. Sometimes an organization's management believes that they can save money by designing a survey internally without outside assistance. The result is almost always a survey that contains many design flaws and that inaccurately collects data. The final results are then usually meaningless but, unfortunately, the same management is blind to the flaws and proceeds to make important judgments and decisions based on flawed data. For your own benefit, **do not try to design a survey questionnaire yourself. Let the professionals do it.**

The Talico Employee Opinion Survey

The *Talico Employee Opinion Survey* (EOS) was developed in the early 1970s by Louis E. Tagliaferri with the assistance of a team of associates and colleagues. The survey instrument (originally titled *The Employee Motivation Survey* with a title change to *The Employee Opinion Survey* in the early 1980s) was developed in a manner fully consistent with accepted social-psychological research methodologies. This means that the instruments has both content and construct validity. Content validity is the extent to which the items comprising the survey instrument sufficiently cover the domain being measured. Construct validity is the assurance that a scale measures what it purports to measure. The instrument has been updated periodically since its development to ensure that survey items measure issues of contemporary importance. In its development every reasonable effort was made to ensure that scale validity was not affected by bias or other such threats as:

> *Social Desirability*: Item wording that uses socially desirable terms which could lead respondents to favor certain response alternatives.

> *Acquiescence*: The tendency of some people to always agree with what would seem to be the "obvious" positive or majority viewpoint.

> *Understandability*: Failure to use language which is familiar and common to respondents when wording survey items.

> *Central Tendency/Extreme Response*: The tendency of some respondents to mark survey responses in a "straight line" manner, i.e. marking all items in the "Agree" column or in the "Strongly Disagree" column.

The EOS use a five-point Likert response scale, the most widely accepted type of response scale. Survey items are worded as statements and require that the respondent express the extent to which they agree or disagree with the statement. Depending on the survey version chosen by the client, either four or five items will comprise a set or measurement dimension. Thus, the measurement dimension "Communication" comprises either four or five statements (items), each item measuring a benchmark attribute of organizational communication. The standard version of the survey consists of 48 items distributed among 12 measurement dimensions. The customized version can have up to 100 items distributed over 20 measurement dimensions (see Appendix C). Both versions offer the option of an unstructured section where employees can write-in comments and suggestions about the work environment.

The Talico EOS has another characteristic of a valid and reliable survey instrument. Normative data are available for all of the 100 survey items in its survey item data bank. A norm is a standard. In the case of an organization climate survey a norm for any survey item is developed by collecting response data over a period of time and then by calculating a weighted average for that item. Most survey data are reported in terms of the percentage of responses to the various response alternatives on a scale. The Talico EOS reports data in terms of response distribution percentages but the focus, as it is in most organization climate surveys, is on the percentage of respondents who respond favorably to a particular survey item. Normative data, therefore, are shown as percentages of positive response. Talico norms are divided into two groups, one for manufacturing related businesses and a second set for service-based organizations. The total normative database consists of responses from over 300,000 employees, approximately 45% manufacturing related and 55% service related.

These survey instrument characteristics, a valid, reliable survey questionnaire supported by normative data, are essential to the success of any organizational climate survey. If you fail to ensure that the core questionnaire of your survey project will accurately and reliably measure the specific attributes that you want to measure within your organization the result could be that you collect a great deal of invalid and useless data that might lead to costly management decision errors. So, we repeat that unless you have staff experienced in survey design **do not try to do it yourself. Let the professionals do it.**

The Survey Process

There are six components to an effective survey process. A **Survey Planning & Administration Guide** that covers each of these phases in detail is presented later in this manual. Below, however, is a short overview that will acquaint the reader with the essentials of the survey process.

Planning

Planning is the keystone of a successful survey project. Included in this phase of the project are activities such as setting specific survey objectives, choosing between a standard or customized survey, determining the scope of the survey, selecting demographic subgroups for reporting purposes, developing a survey communication plan, and deciding the timing and method of survey administration.

Development

In this phase the actual survey questionnaire is prepared either in paper and pencil form or in electronic form on the Internet. In either case draft copies of the questionnaire should be submitted to the client for its approval. After the survey questionnaire is approved by the client it is either printed and shipped to the client or, in the case of an electronic on-line survey, posted on dedicated web site.

Administration

The two most popular methods of survey administration are (1) in traditional paper and pencil format with survey responses marked on a form suitable for optical scanning, and (2) an on-line survey conducted via the Internet. In the former method optimum results are obtained when the survey is administered under proctored conditions to scheduled groups of employees. This ensures maximum employee participation, minimizes the possibility that some employees may collaborate on survey responses to create artificial subgroup response patterns and when accompanied by proper security arrangements this method helps to ensure anonymity and confidentiality of the responses of individual employees (as opposed, for example, to the distribution and collection of survey questionnaires to employees at their work station by their immediate supervisor). On the other hand this survey administration method is somewhat time consuming and requires more "downtime" from work than other methods.

A method of survey administration that is rapidly gaining in popularity is to administer the survey over the Internet. In the case of a Talico EOS a private page is set up for the survey on an Internet site hosted for this purpose. Employees are given the link to the site when the survey is activated and have immediate access to the survey. This is a highly efficient method that enables any employee who has Internet access anywhere in the world to take the survey with complete anonymity and confidentiality at any time of the day. There is very little, if any, "downtime" from work and employees can complete a 48-item Internet survey in about 15 minutes compared with 30 minutes or more when it is in paper and pencil format.

Analysis

However the survey is administered the data collected should be electronically scored and analyzed by survey demographic subgroup. Survey data should also be electronically audited for accuracy and then are reviewed by a survey analysis professional, who assesses and interprets the data, identifies organizational strengths and weaknesses and prepares the survey report. A optional verbatim transcript can be prepared for any write-in comments or suggestions made by employees in the unstructured part of the survey questionnaire.

Reporting

In the case of a Talico survey, a statistical, graphic and narrative report is generated. Samples of typical Talico survey reports, together with guidelines for interpreting survey results, are in the appendix of this manual. These survey reports are designed for clarity and are easily read and interpreted. The chances are that the guidelines will suffice for most survey interpretation needs.

Additional guidance is available via telephone conferencing or other means if required by the client.

The survey report presents a brief Executive Overview that highlights major findings among the statistical data and that includes the All Respondents (organization overall) report, category scores for all demographic subgroups, and analysts observations regarding any survey trends or patterns. The main body of the survey report continues with a presentation of the statistical data for each demographic subgroup and a verbatim transcript of write-in comments, if this option has been selected by the client.

Response Action

There are many reasons why organizations survey their employees. In some cases the objective is simply to obtain a general sense of the current state of employee morale and job satisfaction. But, in most situations management will survey to obtain information that can be used as the basis for various organization improvement programs, ranging from programs to improve organizational communication and building teamwork to those geared toward reducing operating costs or boosting product quality and customer satisfaction. In any case, these organizational improvement efforts can only be achieved if management follows a rational and effective problem-solving process.

Because of the popularity and long history of organization climate survey use in business, industry and government researchers have developed thoroughly tested and proven problem-solving models. These models are typically labeled as *Survey Guided Organization Development* or *Survey Guided Action Planning* or some similar generic term. The appendix of this manual contains a detailed blueprint for survey response action based on this type of model, modified by Talico, so that it can be easily used by the lay person rather than only by survey professionals.

When employees are asked to express their opinions about their job or the work environment they will have certain expectations that management will take some sort of action in response to the needs and concerns that they express. Any management that considers surveying its employees must be prepared to take some meaningful response action as a follow-up. Failure to respond appropriately will very likely have a negative impact on employee morale and in that case it would be better if the survey not been conducted in the first place. This consideration emphasizes the need to establish realistic expectations among employees regarding management's survey intentions in the pre-survey communication phase and also the need for management to respond to survey issues in a manner consistent with responsible business practices.

Survey Planning Guide

This section of the manual presents a detailed plan that contains all of the elements necessary for a successful survey. We have made every effort to simplify the survey process. Still, you should feel free to adapt the plan to the particular circumstances of your organization.

The first step in the survey process is senior management's decision to conduct a survey among your employees. The decision to conduct a survey should be based on the specific objectives that senior management has established for a survey project. This topic was mentioned earlier, but at this point senior management must clearly define what it wants to accomplish by surveying its employees. The survey decision should be based on the consensus of the senior staff. If any key member of senior management withholds his or her full support for the survey then that sentiment will likely filter down through the various functions for which that executive is responsible. Half-hearted support at any level of the organization tends to diminish the full value of the survey but it has an especially deleterious effect on the survey process when it comes from the top. If there any signs of serious reservations about a survey, especially among senior management, then be sure those are fully resolved before proceeding further.

The first thing that you should do after assuring management's commitment to the survey is to lay out a plan. In Appendix A we have included a model Gantt Chart that contains all of the planning elements required for a successful survey. As you may know, a Gantt chart is a project management tool that is used to list projects, subprojects, activities and key or benchmark events. Gantt Charts have been in used by various engineering disciplines for many years. They are very easy to understand and are a highly useful tool that can help project managers both visualize and track the key components of a plan. The sample Gantt chart in Appendix A can serve as a model for a survey project in your organization. The model project is then divided into six subprojects, each subproject being directly related to one of the key phases for a successful survey discussed earlier:

- Planning
- Survey Development and Preparation
- Survey Administration
- Scoring and Analysis
- Reporting and Feedback
- Post-Survey Action Planning

Subprojects are comprised of activities and events. There is a narrow distinction between an activity and an event. As a rule of thumb, an activity usually occurs over a period of time as short as one day or as long as several weeks, while an event is usually a non-recurring situation like a two-hour meeting to make a presentation to senior management. For purposes of simplification we have minimized the number of events and placed more emphasis on activities in the model survey project.

Please take a few minutes to become familiar with the Model Gantt Chart. Study each activity/event, the time duration over which it is scheduled to take place, and the beginning and ending dates, the latter given only for an entire subproject. Note how critical activities or events are linked together to show that they occur in sequence. Also note that the duration of the entire survey project from the appointment of survey facilitators to the presentation of action response plans to management is 158 days. However, 78 of those days concern activities that occur after the survey has been conducted and the survey report has been presented to management. That group of activities is called **Post-Survey Action Planning.** Below is an explanation of what is involved in each of the listed activities or events. Items in bold are major activities.

1.   **Survey Objectives**

Determine the purpose and objectives of the survey.

2. Planning

The purpose of this set of activities is to set a foundation for a successful survey by careful planning and preparation for the survey project.

3.   *Appoint Survey Facilitators*: You should appoint a responsible management level person to serve as your in-house survey facilitator. In the case of the Talico EOS, the facilitator will be the principal contact between our firm and your organization. The facilitator is responsible for coordinating all of the activities that are required for the project, including but not limited to developing a project plan, preparing and disseminating pre-survey communication, reviewing and obtaining approvals for the survey questionnaire, distributing Internet access codes, assisting in the post-survey feedback process and facilitating post-survey problem solving interventions. This is a very important job which should be assigned only to someone who can command the respect of line and staff managers and who has proven project management ability. For purposes of this project the survey facilitator should report to someone on your organization's senior staff, preferably to the chief executive at the surveying location. In locations that have large employee populations it may be advisable to appoint a co-facilitator, as well. Further, some larger organizations appoint a senior management task team to oversee survey activities and in those cases the facilitator reports to that committee.

4.   *Determine the Survey Scope*: One decision that you must make is whether you will survey the entire population or only a statistical sample. In most cases the latter is not a viable option for several reasons. The statistical validity of data from the sampling method of surveying is a function of the size of the population in which the sample is taken and of the sample size. The problem centers on the fact that your survey is divided into demographic subgroups for analytical purposes. These subgroups will almost certainly be of unequal size and some of them may be relatively small. Thus, the statistical validity of the data may not be equal among the various subgroups and in the smaller subgroups you would need to sample almost 100% anyway in order to obtain valid data. But in addition, experience has shown that employees tend to disfavor sampling. Many who are selected as part of a sample suspiciously question why they were selected while many of those who were not selected are unhappy that they cannot participate. In most cases sampling is a "lose-lose" proposition. We strongly recommend, therefore, that all employees in the target population be surveyed.

But, that brings up another survey scope issue. What should comprise the target population? For example, will you be surveying either hourly and salaried employees or only one of those groups? How about off-site employees, part-time employees and any contractor employees who may work either full or part-time at your location but who are not actually on your payroll? There is no guideline for these decisions because each surveying organization has its own unique set of circumstances. Nonetheless, these issues are an important part of your decision about the scope of the survey.

5. *Select Demographic Subgroups*: By demographics we mean the subgroup breakouts that you will need for analysis purposes in addition to an organization overall or "All Respondents" report. Here are the most typical kinds of demographic subgroups that most organizations choose:

- *Region or Facility* like Southwest Region or Cleveland Operation,
- *Departments* like Accounting, Project Management or Designers,
- *Functions* like Managers, Technical & Professional, Hourly, or Clerical,
- *Status* like Exempt or Non-exempt or Minority or Part-time,
- *Length of Service* like 5-10 Years or 20 Years Plus

Some organizations like hospitals will have many subgroups while others will have very few. The general rule is to have as few as possible without sacrificing the meaningfulness of the survey data that will be collected. Too few subgroups may inhibit management's ability to pinpoint areas within the organization where morale and job satisfaction may be very high or where there may be serious problems. On the other hand, too many subgroups can quickly lead to information overload making it very cumbersome and difficult to evaluate the survey data. The Talico EOS includes up to 10 subgroups as a standard feature but it can accommodate any number that the client may choose. Your job is to determine which particular demographic subgroup reports will be suitable for your organization.

6. *Determine the Survey Method*: As explained earlier the two most common methods for conducting a survey are the traditional "paper and pencil" method and the newer Internet method. The pros and cons of each of these methods have already been discussed. If you are considering the Internet survey method you can see a sample of how a typical survey is posted on our Internet site by going to the following Internet address: www.talico.com. Accessing an online is very easy for employees. At the time that the survey is activated employees are provided by a hyperlink that takes them directly to the survey on a private and confidential page at Internet survey site. More about this procedure later.

   The typical lead time to set up an Internet survey is only about 2 weeks. It is about 3 to 4 weeks for a "paper and pencil" survey. The reason for this is that in the former once we know what survey items and categories you want we simply post them on the Internet page and give you the access code so that you can quickly review and approve the questionnaire. However, a traditional survey requires the set up of a print master, the exchange of print proofs and finally the printing and shipping of the paper questionnaires. Once in your hands it is your responsibility to distribute and collect the paper-based survey questionnaires and return them to us (by insured, traceable express means, please). We will help you to set a schedule for the individual events in either version.

7. *Prepare a Survey Communication Plan*: The survey communication plan is one of the more important activities in the survey project. Timely, accurate

and credible two-way communication between management and employees is absolutely essential to survey success. Most initial communication about the survey will be directed from management to the employees. But, even during this period it is important that management obtain feedback from employees so that it can answer any questions that they might have about the survey process, reassure them that the survey results will be used constructively and also ensure that they know their individual survey responses will be completely anonymous and confidential. Components of the survey communication plan include:

- pre-survey announcements to all employees,
- survey access instructions and procedures,
- survey administration period reminders,
- end of survey administration period memo,
- survey report receipt memo,
- survey results feedback meetings,
- on-going post-survey communication.

More information about the survey communication plan, including sample memos and letters, will be found in Appendix B.

8. Survey Questionnaire Development

The purpose of this set of activities is to design a questionnaire (for either traditional or Internet application) that fully meets your survey requirements and to prepare to administer it among your employees by the most practicable and effective method for your organization.

9. *Design the Survey Questionnaire*: The actual items on either an Internet survey or a "paper and pencil" survey are the same. It is just the method of administration that is different. Appendix C contains a list of pre-designed 100 items that are available for any Talico EOS. These items are distributed among 20 measurement dimensions. You can pick and choose among these item sets to select those most appropriate items for your

survey. If you believe that you have special survey needs that are not quite met by the 100 items we can help you to tailor the questionnaire to meet your exact survey requirements.

10. *Obtain Approvals*: After you have selected the categories and items for your survey we will either post the questionnaire on the Internet or prepare printing proofs. In either case we will notify you when you can review the draft questionnaire to ensure its accuracy. We request signed approvals from your survey facilitator before we either post or print the final version of the questionnaire. Of course, your survey facilitator should first obtain internal approvals from senior management before "signing off" on the questionnaire and other material himself or herself. Our reference to the questionnaire includes any accompanying material such as survey instructions or procedures that will be distributed to employees and demographic subgroup information.

11. *Select and Train Survey Administrators*: In-house survey administrators will be needed only in the event that you choose to conduct a proctored traditional survey. The function of the survey administrator is to distribute survey questionnaires, read the survey instructions to employees, make sure that employees have a sufficient supply of pencils or pens, monitor the survey to ensure that employees are completing the questionnaire without collaborating with other employees and then collect the completed questionnaires and scan forms. Ideally, in-house survey administrators should be Human Resource staff members or other employees who are perceived by employees to be neutral, i.e., a staff that is not part of the line management to which the employees being surveyed directly report. Survey administrators may clarify survey procedures to employees but they must be careful not to suggest how employees should respond to survey items.

12. *Prepare Survey Material*: This is a responsibility of the survey consultant that should be coordinated with your in-house survey facilitator.

13. Administer the Survey

The purpose of this set of activities is data collection. It involves conducting the survey among your employees, encouraging optimum participation in the survey, and gathering and consolidating the survey data once survey questionnaires have been completed or the Internet posting period has been closed.

14. *Conduct the Survey*: In the case of a proctored traditional "paper and pencil" survey employees should be scheduled to take the survey in a meeting or conference room in groups of from 10 to preferably no more than 25. Survey administration meetings can be held at hourly intervals in most cases. This will allow sufficient time for the survey administrator to introduce the survey, distribute questionnaires, read the survey instructions, allow time for survey completion and collect the completed survey questionnaires. Proctored surveys generally have an 80% to 95% participation rate.

One way to reinforce that individual survey results are completely anonymous is to prepare a large sealed box with a ballot-like slot on one side. The box should be pre-addressed and labeled for return to the survey data scoring center. After the employees have completed their questionnaire they insert the separate scan from into the survey booklet and then drop the booklet into the slot in the box. The last employee who completes the survey is asked to seal the slot and the box is then immediately put into the out-going express shipment system. If you prefer you can request that one or more employees witness the box pick up by FEDEX or whatever express carrier you have selected. There are also other methods and alternative ways to help safeguard the anonymity and confidentiality of the employees' responses to the survey.

An Internet survey is, of course, conducted in a much different way. In order for you to conduct an Internet survey employees must have access to a computer with an Internet connection. In modern service industry businesses and in much of government it is common for the majority of employees to use a computer for one reason or another. Non-production employees in many manufacturing businesses likewise generally have ready computer access. Even many of those employees who do not regularly use a computer at work have one at home and in most cases they have Internet access on their home computer. Beyond these considerations, it is quite easy for most organizations to set up a number of computers with Internet access in a meeting or conference room for the convenience of those employees who may not otherwise have one available. If none of these conditions apply to your organization then you should conduct a traditional survey and not one on the Internet.

You were familiarized with the Talico Online Employee Opinion Survey process earlier in this manual. Sample memos to employees with instructions for accessing an Internet survey are included in Appendix B. There are several other aspects of conducting an Internet survey that you should consider, however. First, many organizations have a "firewall" in their computer system both to prevent someone from outside the organization accessing their computer system without authorization and also to prevent employees from "surfing" the Internet without authorization. Your computer system specialist can easily develop a temporary program that allows your employees to access only our Internet site for survey purposes. When the survey is completed that portal is closed.

Confidentially and anonymity of individual response is very strongly maintained in an Internet survey. Our systems ensure that no individual who participates in a Talico EOS can be identified by their responses. While your survey facilitator will be allowed to access part of our system to obtain a daily count of the number of employees who responded to the survey, that person will not have access to the actual response file.

Next, there is the issue of how long the survey should be posted in order to obtain optimum employee response. We suggest two weeks. Longer periods are possible but experience indicates that with reminder memos a two-week posting period should produce a 70% to 80% participation rate. The nature of an Internet survey is such that employees can take the survey from anywhere in the world at anytime of the day. This is an especially desirable feature when an organization has a field sales or engineering force or when the nature of their business requires frequent travel for executives, technical and professional employees.

It is unlikely that employees will experience any difficulty accessing the Talico Internet site to take the survey. But, from time to time conditions beyond our control do occur. For example, a few years ago a massive power outage in the mid-Atlantic states caused a short shutdown of the main server until the auxiliary power source "kicked in." That condition was promptly remedied but a couple of employees from the mid-west could not access the site during that time. When we give you the access code for your employees we also give you a technical services telephone number for employees to call in the event that they have difficulty of any technical nature accessing the survey from their computer station. If they need help a technical person will assist them as soon as possible.

15. *Consolidate the Survey Responses*: Gathering the data from various survey locations and consolidating it into a single database suitable for scoring and analysis.

16. Scoring and Analysis:

The purpose of this set of activities is to score the raw survey data, sort the scored data into the various demographic subgroups, analyze the results to identify any significant trends or patterns and to prepare a report of survey findings.

17.   *Score the Survey Data*: Paper form surveys are optically scanned and then are electronically scored by Talico using proprietary survey scoring software. Survey data from Internet files are collected and scored using similar software.

18.   *Audit the Raw Data*: The purpose of this activity is to identify any survey data anomalies in relation to the known survey population and response rate.

19.   *Analyze Survey Results*: Survey scores are electronically sorted by demographic subgroup. The data are then reviewed by a Talico professional to identify significant findings.

20.   *Prepare the Survey Report*: The final survey report consists of an executive overview that calls attention to major survey findings in narrative, tabular and graphic form, statistical analyses of the scores in each subgroup and for the organization overall, and a verbatim transcript of any write-in comments made by employees. Verbatim means that the comments are presented in raw form without editing for content, grammar, spelling or punctuation.

21.   Reporting and Feedback

      The purposes of this set of activities are to submit the survey report to the organization's senior management, ensure that the survey data are clearly understood and properly interpreted, process the data among key executives and managers, and communicate a summary of survey results to employees.

22.   *Submit the Survey Report to Management*: A final survey report is submitted to your senior management within 2-3 weeks of our receipt of the completed survey questionnaires, in the case of a traditional survey, or the end of the posting period for an Internet Survey. Management receives one bound copies of the report and a file in Adobe Acrobat 5.0 or higher so that it can reproduce and distribute additional reports.

23. *Conduct First Management Review Meeting*: As soon as possible after receipt of the survey report the senior management of your organization should meet to review the major survey findings. Before that meeting the survey facilitator should ensure that all senior management executives have had an opportunity to read relevant sections of this manual. For example, in Appendix D we present a sample survey report together with an explanation of the report format and guidelines that are very helpful for purposes of analyzing and interpreting the survey data in its various forms. All members of senior management should read at least that section of this manual before they begin reviewing the survey report.

We suggest that the focus at this initial report review meeting be on assessing the overall organizational climate. This will involve first a thorough study of the data in the Executive Overview, including the All Respondents statistical report. It should also include a review of the Survey Category statistical reports for each of the various major demographic subgroups. What is a major subgroup to one organization may not be the same for another organization. However, we believe that the most important subgroups are regions or branches, departments and principal job functions.

Meeting participants should note any major variances in category scores between the organization's overall data (All Respondents Report) and the category scores of the various subgroups. It would be too ponderous and confusing a task to attempt to compare individual item scores among the subgroups at this time. That should be left for later meetings after each senior executive has had a chance to review the data that pertains to his or her area of responsibility in sufficient detail.

After the first management review meeting there should be an incubation period of a few days to no more than two weeks. But before adjourning the first meeting senior management should prepare communication to employees in which the latter are informed that the survey report has been received by senior management and that it is now studying the survey results. Employees should be told that they will receive further information about the survey results at a date to be announced. The communication should conclude by senior management expressing its sincere appreciation to employees for their candid and helpful opinions and it should reassure them that management intends to respond to survey issues in a constructive way. Appendix B contains a sample memo for this purpose that can be sent out through the organization's regular communication channels.

24. *Conduct the Second Management Review Meeting*: Having allowed a few days' incubation period, senior management should now reconvene for a working session. Before this meeting is convened, though, the full survey report should be shared with all members of the senior management decision making team. When this team convenes it should first poll its members for any feelings of sensing that they might have about the survey data as it applies both to the organization overall and also to the various demographic subgroups. This sensing should be openly discussed and any general questions answered to the extent possible. Referring to the survey data, the team should then begin to process the data by making a list of major strengths and weaknesses, distinguishing between systemic and local issues and other problem solving tasks, all of which are detailed in Appendix D. In most cases senior management will require from one to three additional problem solving meetings to complete these tasks. Some organizations prefer to condense the process and hold an off-site problem solving retreat for this purpose. It is often helpful to retain an organizational development specialist to facilitate meetings of this type.

25. *Communicate Survey Results to Employees*: This is the final step before beginning the Post-Survey Action Planning activity set. Some organizations take the survey process no further than this (including, of course, management's own problem solving activities as listed earlier). It is very important that employees be informed about significant survey findings. Failure to do so would have a serious negative impact on management credibility and on the credibility of the entire exercise.

It is not necessary that management share the survey data with employees in the same detail that it was presented in the final survey report. For example, the survey report contains detailed subgroup analyses with tabulations, graphics and statistical response distributions. First, much of these data would be "over the heads" of the average employees. Secondly, as a general rule management should not distribute anything to employees that it would not want released to the public. This is a very important point because disgruntled employees have been known to send copies of detailed survey data both to the press and to customers when this information was made available to them in written form.

Instead, management is advised to "keep it simple." An honest and objective summary of the major survey issues, both positive and negative, in a simple chart or list will suffice quite well. We recommend that if at all possible this summary be presented to employees in group meetings rather than in paper or electronic form. Ideally these meetings would be held in an auditorium or large conference room, a facility that could accommodate 50 or more employees at one sitting. The meeting duration need be only 20 to 30 minutes. It should be introduced by the survey facilitator and the information should be presented by a member of the senior staff. Overhead projections or computer graphics can be used to enhance the presentation and highlight main points.

Employees should be informed at the opening of the meeting that its purpose is to give them feedback about the survey data. Although at the end of the presentation there should be a brief question and answer period, it should be remembered that the purpose of the meeting is on-way communication and therefore no attempt should be made at trying to encourage an extensive discussion about the data or its meaning. If you intend to proceed later to Post-Survey Action Planning, which by its nature involves employees in the process, then you can use this occasion to inform them about that process. If you have not selected that activity then at the very least you should tell employees that you will use regular communication channels to keep them informed about any action management will take in response to survey issues.

26.   Post-Survey Action Planning

The purpose of this set of activities is to, validate and clarify the statistical survey data, obtain additional information about employees' job related perceptions, involve employees in the post-survey problem solving process, and to develop and implement specific strategies for dealing with priority survey issues.

27   *Appoint Focus Groups*: The first step in the post-survey action planning process is to gather additional data about employees' attitudes, opinions and other job related beliefs and perceptions. This includes the validation of the statistical data and write-in comments in the survey. In order to do this it is necessary to share and discuss certain survey results with employees. Some organizations have conducted one-on-one interviews with employees for this purpose. However, we have found that method to be the least desirable way to obtain additional data. Even when an outside specialist is used to conduct one-on-one interviews employees often feel intimidated by the process, even when the selection process is truly random as it should be. Many are guarded and less than candid in their responses to interview questions. Because of this consideration and also because of the potential benefits of group dynamics we strongly recommend that focus groups be appointed for post-survey data interview purposes.

For the purpose of this type of intervention, focus groups will be homogeneous, consisting of from six to 10 employees selected at random from a common demographic subgroup – preferably from a common work unit. Groups consisting of less than six employees tend to be monopolized by one or two employees, while those larger than 10 often tend to inhibit full participation by all members in part by group size.

The number of focus groups to be selected is a function of survey results. Focus groups should definitely be appointed from subgroups where significant problem issues were identified in the survey. But, there is also merit in appointing two or more focus groups from those subgroups that had mostly high survey scores. This way more accurate clarification and validation of survey results will be possible. Some organizations have even formed focus groups among all of their employees. However, conducting focus group interviews is a very labor intensive process. Management is advised to be practical when it decides how many are necessary in order to obtain the desired results. (Guidelines for conducting focus group interviews are included in Appendix E.)

28. *Appoint and Train Focus Group Facilitators*: Candidly, very few employees within a surveying organization will have the skill to conduct meaningful and productive focus group interviews. The meeting facilitator must be proficient in the skills of meeting leadership, group process and indirect questioning, to name just a few skills. At the same time, he or she must be knowledgeable about the meaning and interpretation of the survey data and be able to synthesize one bit of information from one employee with another bit from another employee. In larger organizations certain human resource professionals may have this skill (certain of the skills are the same that they must use when interviewing employees for employment, for example). But, most organizations will be best advised to retain a behavioral science professional for this purpose. In turn, that professional can conduct in-house training sessions where he or she can instruct management level employees from the surveying organization in required methods and techniques so that the entire focus group process can be expedited.

What must be strictly avoided is for overly-confident managers to conduct focus group meetings without the proper training. There are many traps that these people can fall into such as dominating the meeting themselves, not ensuring full inclusion in the discussion, not being able to handle challenges or difficult questions from employees, expressing their own opinions about the survey results and much more.

29. *Conduct the Focus Group Interviews*: See Appendix E.

30. *Summarize and Analyze Focus Group Data*: After the focus group interviews have been completed, the data and information from those meetings must be summarized and analyzed. Any information that either supports and validates or contradicts the data and information in the survey should be highlighted. So should data or information that while neither validating nor contradicting survey findings helps to explain the reasons for employees' responses. As in the survey itself, care must be taken to preserve the confidentiality and anonymity of input form individual employees. Therefore, the summarization of the focus group meetings should be screened to eliminate identifying comments or situations.

31. *Submit an Addendum Report to Management*: The findings from all focus group interview meetings should be prepared in report form including any appropriate tabulations or graphics, such as bar or pie charts, and then should be submitted to senior management. The data and information in this addendum report should be categorized by demographic subgroup and, if the meetings were sufficiently extensive, for the organization overall. The person who prepares the report must be careful to avoid generalizing conclusions that are in fact relevant only to one or more demographics to the organization as a whole. This report, when submitted, becomes a very important part of the overall information decision base that senior management obtains from the survey project.

32. *Conduct Work Unit Problem Solving Interventions*: At this point senior management should have all of the data and information that it needs to begin addressing survey issues. You will recall that in the reporting and feedback activity set one task for senior management was to sort problem issues into two categories: *systemic* issues common to the organization as a whole, and *local* issues that are unique or relevant to only certain individual subgroups. A senior management task team should be

appointed to deal with systemic problems while it should be the responsibility of individual subgroup management to deal with survey issues relevant to their areas of responsibility.

There are several models that you can use as the basis for these problem solving efforts. One of the best is called creative problem solving, a technique that makes use of both convergent and divergent thinking. It helps you to more clearly define problem solving issues and to bring both rational (scientific) and creative methodologies to bear on finding the most effective solutions. It should be left up to the problem solving teams to decide which methods they prefer and whether to use a team approach or to assign competent individual contributors to solve certain problems. We prefer the team approach because it can produce synergistic results. Whichever methods are selected, deadlines should be set for the individual problem solving teams to present their findings and action plans to senior management. Problem solving time lines vary widely depending on the organization, the nature of the problems, the skills of the problem solving teams and other considerations. This period could range from as little as two weeks to as long as three months. You must decide what is best for your organization.

33. *Present Action Plans to Management*: At the end of the problem solving period the various teams summarize their efforts, prepare a report of their findings and present their recommendations to senior management. We recommend that if you extend your survey to this set of activities you conclude them with personal team presentations. There are many benefits to this approach, not the least of which is that it visibly demonstrates that senior management is continuing to listen and seriously consider input from employees about ways to improve morale and organization effectiveness. It is also an excellent opportunity for senior management to gain a first-hand assessment of the team effectiveness, analytical skills and other problem solving abilities of various managers, supervisors and rank-and-file employees.

34.	*Implement Action Plans*: The final activity of the survey process is to implement approved action plans. For the most part the responsibility for implementing survey response action is with line management. The implementation process should include appropriate control measures to ensure that the objectives of the plans are being met according to the plan schedule and that the desired results are being realized. All plans should include measurement criteria by which the success of the plans can be evaluated. In most cases it is possible to begin implementing survey response action about six months after a survey is conducted. Results begin appearing about six months after implementation. Because of this we suggest that any re-surveys to measure progress be conducted not less than 12 months nor longer than 24 months after the initial survey.

Conclusion

There is one final thought about organization climate surveys that should be discussed. A survey is much like a financial balance sheet. It is a snapshot of a condition at a particular point in time. Like a balance sheet, survey data not only can but almost certainly will change with time. Also, like the financial picture that a balance sheet portrays, the organization climate data that a survey portrays is affected by many variables.

In both business and government changes in senior management often are accompanied by changes in organization policy and practice. A new senior management might either embrace or reject the policies and practices of the former management. It is not uncommon, therefore, for an organization to embark on a program of organization change or renewal only to have that program halted or modified by the next generation of policy makers. This type of structural volatility can have a significant impact on employees' perceptions, for better or worse, and thus on their survey responses from one period to another. Another source of perception volatility is the quality of the employees' immediate manger or supervisor. That is one reason why organization climate surveys are also highly useful tools for identifying possible skill or behavioral development needs among managers and supervisors.

Lastly, there is the continuing debate about the extent that a "people metric" can relate in a meaningful way to an organization's "bottom line." Studies have long shown that in most cases there is a significant correlation between employee morale and job satisfaction and certain indirect performance indices like labor turnover, the quality of labor relations (including grievance volume, arbitration and even on the outcome of labor negotiations in unionized organizations) and even job safety indices. Historically the correlations have been much less meaningful when applied to the relationship between morale and job satisfaction and direct performance measures.

This is still the case if one attempts to correlate a broadly defined term like job satisfaction with an index like customer satisfaction or labor productivity or earnings per share. The reason for this is that in many organizations other variables like the design and structure of a job (including how closely employees must follow well-defined procedures rather than be allowed to exercise independent judgment) and technology have a far greater impact on organization performance than employee morale and job satisfaction. But, most recently it has been found that there is indeed a certain core of job-related attributes that do correlate closely with bottom line performance measures. These attributes include the extent that employees:

- believe that senior management is in control of conditions that determine business success,

- believe that senior management is operating the business effectively,

- are confident in the credibility of senior management communication,

- believe that they are producing or performing a meaningful product or service,

- have confidence in the quality of the product or service that they produce or perform, know what is expected of them in quantitative and qualitative terms,

- know how well they are meeting those expectations,

- possess the training, skills and abilities to meet perform their jobs effectively, and more.

These and certain other job related attributes can be measured by a properly structured organization climate survey. They not only relate to organization performance but also they can help predict it. Our own studies of survey results for clients have established correlations as high as .62 among certain of the above attribute and organization performance criteria. That is one reason why organization climate surveys can help speed business recovery from the recent recessionary period and why informed senior executives are more frequently including organization climate surveys in their arsenal of decision making tools.

Appendix A
Model EOS Project Schedule

Start: 03/18/02
Finish: 10/24/02

Sample : EOS Project Schedule
Outline Gantt View: Default Outline Gantt View Table

Page #1

	Activity Name	Duration	2002 02	03	Q2-2002 04	05	06	Q3-2002 07	08	09	Q4-2002 10	11	12	Q1-2003 01	02
1	⊟ EOS Project Schedule	158	03/18/02								10/23/02				
2	⊟ General Planning	10	03/18/02	03/29/02											
3	Appoint & Train Facilitators	2	03/18/02												
4	Select Demographic Subgroups	3	03/20/02												
5	Prepare Communication Plan	5	03/25/02												
6	⊟ Questionnaire Development	10	03/25/02	04/05/02											
7	Review & Modify Questionnaire	3	03/25/02												
8	Obtain Approvals	2	03/28/02												
9	Post on Internet	3	04/01/02												
10	Final Review & Approval	2	04/04/02												
11	⊟ Survey Administration	15		04/10/02	04/30/02										
12	Release Access Codes	2		04/10/02											
13	Conduct Survey	10		04/12/02											
14	Consolidate & Audit Data	3		04/26/02											
15	⊟ Scoring & Analysis	7			05/02/02 05/10/02										
16	Score Survey Data	3			05/02/02										
17	Audit Data	1			05/07/02										
18	Analyze Survey Scores	3			05/08/02										
19	⊟ Report Prep & Presentation	23			05/13/02	06/12/02									
20	Generate Survey Report	5			05/13/02										
21	Present Survey Report to Mgt	3			05/20/02										
22	First Mgt Review	5			05/23/02										
23	Communicate Results to Employes	5			05/30/02										
24	Second Mgt Review	5			06/06/02										
25	⊟ Post-Survey Action Planning	78					07/08/02			10/23/02					
26	Appoint & Train Focus Groups Ldrs	5					07/08/02								
27	Appoint Focus Groups	3					07/15/02								
28	Conduct Focus Group Meetings	10					07/18/02								
29	Summarize & Analyze FG Results	5						08/01/02							
30	Submit Sup. Report to Mgt	5						08/08/02							
31	Conduct Prob Solv Interventions	15						08/15/02							
32	Present Action Plans to Mgt	5							09/05/02						
33	Implement Approved Action Plans	30							09/12/02						

Project	Start (Early) ◁▭▷ Finish (Early)	Non Crit. Activity	Start (Early) ▭ Resource Names
Subproject	Start (Early) ◁▭▷ Finish (Early)	Event	Start (Early) ▽ Name
Critical Activity	Start (Early) ▭ Resource Names	Interface Event	Start (Early) ◆ Name

▓ Non-Cum. Actual Profile   ▨ Non-Cum. Remaining Profile   Non-Cum. Baseline Profile   Cum. Act.+Rem. Profile   Cum. Baseline Profile

Filtered by objects: <All Objects>, usages: and Sorted by <None>

Print Date 03/20/03

Appendix B
Survey Communication Plan

Sample Pre-Survey Announcement #1

To All Employees:

The interest and welfare of all of our employees have always been a matter of special importance to me. Because of this I am pleased to announce that during the week of _____ we will conduct an employee opinion survey with the principal objective of finding ways to make _____ an even better place to work.

Full details about the survey, which will be conducted with the assistance of Talico Developmental Systems, L.C., an experienced survey research firm, will be announced shortly. However, information obtained from the survey will be used to help:

1.   improve communication between employees at all organizational levels,

2.   improve the skills of our employees, especially in the areas of teamwork and interpersonal relations,

3.   identify and, wherever practicable, correct any causes of employee dissatisfaction, and

4.   obtain feedback and suggestions from employees about ways that we can improve the effectiveness of our operations and the overall performance of our organization.

I hope that all employees participate fully in the survey and I assure you that your individual responses to the survey questions will be strictly anonymous and confidential.

Sincerely,

Sample Pre-Survey Announcement #2

To All Employees:

During the week of _____ we will be conducting an employee opinion survey in order to learn what your feelings, ideas and suggestions are about your job, the work environment here at _____, management and supervisory practices, the quality of communication and other matters affecting both employee satisfaction and morale and the quality of service that we provide our customers.

The survey, which has been used nationwide by many businesses and industries, will be conducted by Talico Developmental Systems, L.C., an experienced survey research firm. It is easy to complete and offers you a good method by which you can express your opinions and concerns with complete anonymity. **You will not be personally identified in the survey**. Survey data will be collected only on the basis of department and job function and when the survey is completed the survey research firm will provide our senior management with a statistical summary of that data.

A schedule of group meetings has been given to your department head who will inform you when you can take the survey, which requires only about 35 minutes to complete. Your opinions and suggestions are very important to us and I hope that you will fully participate in the survey project. Thank you.

Sincerely,

Sample Pre-Survey Announcement #3 (Internet Survey)

To All Employees

It has long been my personal belief that the employees of this organization are its most valuable assets. It is the dedicated, high quality individual and team contribution of our employees that has helped this organization achieve business success and retain our competitive position, especially during these very challenging times.

Because of this I am pleased to announce a new initiative that will improve our ability to listen and respond to the interests, needs and concerns of our employees. The first phase of this initiative is a survey of the attitudes and opinions of all _____ employees that will be conducted by Talico Developmental Systems L.C. (TDS), a survey research firm, during the two week period beginning _____ . Because all of our employees have access to a computer, the survey will be taken entirely over the Internet on a private and confidential web page that TDS will post on its Internet site. Results from the survey will be used as a data base for the development of organizational improvement programs that we will develop and implement over the next twelve to eighteen months.

Complete details about how you can participate in the survey will be e-mailed to you soon. In the meanwhile I want to personally assure you that your individual responses to survey questions will be strictly anonymous and confidential. Further, after we in senior management have received and studied the survey report, we will share a summary of major survey findings with all employees and request employee involvement in the action planning process that is a key part of this strategic initiative.

Sincerely,

Sample Pre-Survey Announcement #4 (Mail-in Survey)

To All Field Sales and Off-Site Employees

As previously announced we are conducting an employee opinion survey for all employees next week. A notice has been posted informing employees here at the Division as to the time their work group is scheduled to take the survey and the conference room where the survey will be administered. However, for those of you who are field sales or other off-site employees the survey will be conducted via the mail.

Enclosed is a survey booklet containing the survey questions accompanied by an optical scoring sheet for your responses to survey items. Please read the survey instructions carefully. Then complete the survey questionnaire (**do not sign it**), place it in the enclosed, self-addressed, stamped envelope and mail it not later than _____ directly to Talico Developmental Systems, L.C., the survey research firm that will analyze the responses and send a statistical summary report to management.

I assure you that your individual survey responses will be anonymous and you will not personally be identified in any way. Further, we will use the survey results solely for the purpose of improving our organization as a place to work and for improving the effectiveness of our entire Divisional team.

Sincerely,

Sample Survey Scheduling Memo (Non-Internet)

To: All Employees

From: Tom Baker, Director of Human Resources

Two weeks ago John Smith, vice president of operations, announced that we would soon be conducting an employee opinion survey. The survey has now been scheduled for the week of October 15th. Survey administration meetings will be held in Conference Room B which can comfortably accommodate about 30 employees at one time.

The survey will be administered by Haley Svendsen of our human resources department. Haley will distribute survey booklets to employees, provide instructions regarding how they can be completed and answer any procedural questions that might arise. She will also ensure that all completed survey questionnaires are placed in secure shipping packets that will be sealed and sent directly to the survey research firm at the end of each day during the survey period. Absolutely no one from our organization will ever see or otherwise have access to the completed survey questionnaires. Individual responses are anonymous and will be held in strict confidence by the survey research firm.

A schedule of survey administration times will be posted on the bulletin board in each department. Please check the bulletin board to see when your work group is scheduled to attend a survey session. Participation in the survey is voluntary. However, your interests, concerns and suggestions are important to us and we hope that you will participate in the survey by candidly expressing your opinions. Thank you in advance for helping us in this very worthwhile project.

Sample E-Mail Internet Survey Instructions

In my E-Memo dated _____ I informed you that the _____ Operation has been selected to participate in an employee opinion survey, the first phase of a corporate-wide strategic initiative designed to improve the work environment and operating effectiveness here at _____ . The purpose of this memo is to provide you with instructions for accessing and responding to the Talico Online Employee Opinion Survey™ that will be used for this project.

The survey will be conducted by Talico Developmental Systems, L.C. (Talico). Talico is an independent survey research firm that we have selected to be our vendor for this project. The survey will be available on a private and confidential Internet page that is posted on the web site of Talico's Internet survey host from (*Insert Dates*). In order to participate in the survey you can use any Internet-connected computer, whether at work or at home or even a laptop computer if you are traveling. All you need to do is to follow the steps listed below:

1. Go to the following Internet address: (*Insert URL that Talico will provide here*). This link will take you directly to the survey page that will introduce you the survey.

2. **The survey contains 48 items in the form of statements, pull down menu boxes that contain demographic information that will be used for statistical purposes only and one open-ended item.** Your individual responses to the survey are anonymous and confidential and will not identify you personally in any way. The raw survey data will never be seen by anyone from this organization. Only Talico survey professionals will have access to that data and they will hold it strictly confidential.

3. The online instructions to the survey will explain how you can use your cursor to respond to the various survey items. For your general information, the survey items are arranged in sets of 10

with each set being separated by a page. In order to advance to the next set of questions simply click on the "Next" button at the bottom of each page. It is an easy and effective way for you to let us know what your opinions are about important aspects of your job and the work environment in this organization.

As you complete the survey questionnaire think of the term "management" as being the management of the _____ Operation, the term "organization" to mean the _____ Operation and the term "supervisor" to mean your immediate supervisor.

It will take you only about 15 minutes to complete the survey. Remember, our goal is to have a 100% employee participation in this project and your responses are very important to us. Thank you in advance for your participation.

Sincerely,

Daniel Ardito
VP Operations

P.S. If you have any questions about the survey or if you encounter any problems when you are entering responses please contact Eric Svendsen in the Human Resources department.

Sample Reminder for Internet Surveys

Have you Logged On Yet?

There Are Only 3 More Survey Days Left!

**Your Opinions and Suggestions Are Very
Important. Please Participate In
The Online Employee Opinion Survey.**

Go to: www.talico.com/online/EOS
Enter the access code:

**It Will Take Only About 15 Minutes of
Your Time and We Need Your Feedback!**

Thank You!

Sample Survey Report Receipt Memo

To All Employees

We have just received the confidential Employee Opinion Survey report from the survey research firm. This report is now being reviewed by me and by all of my senior staff. The report contains a statistical summary of survey results and a transcript of employees' write-in comments in anonymous form.

As soon as the senior management staff completes its study of the survey data we will prepare a summary of major survey findings which will be communicated to all employees through departmental meetings. Your immediate supervisor will inform you when a survey feedback meeting will be held for your work group. In the meanwhile, I want to personally thank each of you for your participation in the survey project. Over 95% of our employees took the survey and it is already clear that input from employees was constructive and meaningful. You can be certain that we in management will use the survey results in a responsible manner for the mutual benefit of both our employees and of our organization.

Sincerely,

Sample Survey Feedback Meeting Notice

To All Employees In Department 16

A series of feedback meetings in which results of the recent Employee Opinion Survey will be presented will be held on March 10th in the main cafeteria. Your immediate supervisor will set up a schedule which will allow all Department 16 employees to attend one of the meetings on that day. The schedule will be posted on the department bulletin board by Friday of this week.

Sample Focus Group Notice

To All Employees

As part of our continuing efforts to process the data and information from the recent Employee Opinion Survey, we will be holding a series of focus group meetings during the week of November 8th. The purpose of these meetings is to clarify certain issues of concern that employees expressed in the survey, to obtain a better understanding about work environment strengths and weaknesses, and to obtain more detailed suggestions from employees about what can be done to remedy problem areas and to further build on our strengths.

Each focus group meeting will have from 8 to 10 employees selected entirely at random from each department. The meetings will last from one hour to one and one-half hour each. Participation is strictly voluntary. If you are selected but choose not to participate just candidly tell us. However, we believe that those employees selected for the meetings will find it to be a meaningful and rewarding experience.

We have retained an outside management consultant to facilitate the focus group meetings. This person is experienced in the post-survey action planning process and will ensure both that the meetings are as productive as possible and at the same time that the responses of individual employees are kept completely confidential and anonymous. Absolutely no members of management or supervision will attend a focus group meeting that is also attended by their subordinates.

Invitations to attend one of the focus group meetings will be sent out by the end of this week. Thank you again for your continued support of our efforts to improve the work environment here at the _____ Division.

Sincerely,

**Appendix C
Survey Item List**

TDS SURVEY ITEM SETS

The following item sets and individual items are the copyrighted property of the author and the proprietary property of Talico Developmental Systems L.C. They may not be reproduced or used in any manner or by any means without the express written permission of the author and Talico Developmental Systems L.C.

01. Communication

01.1   Communication from the leadership of this organization is open and honest.
01.2   Employees here are free to speak up and say what they think.
01.3   I get all of the information that I need to do my job properly.
01.4   My supervisor/team leader is an accurate, reliable source of information.
01.5   Decision making information is properly shared among those who need it.

02. Compensation & Benefits

02.1   The pay rate for my job has been properly set.
02.2   I am personally paid fairly for the type of work I do.
02.3   Pay increases are administered fairly and consistently.
02.4   I have a good understanding about my employee benefit plan.
02.5   The employee benefit plan here meets my needs satisfactorily.

03. Customer Service

03.1   This organization tries to meet all of its customers' needs and expectations.
03.2   Learning about the satisfaction of our customers is a top priority.

03.3   Feedback from our customers is used to improve product and service quality.
03.4   We have an effective process for responding to customer complaints or problems.
03.5   We are equally committed to satisfy the needs and expectations of our internal customers (employees in other departments and work groups).

04. Cultural Diversity

04.1 Employees of all cultures are made to feel welcome in this organization.

04.2 Any inter-cultural relations issues that may arise here are properly handled.

04.3 In my work group we seldom experience incidents of inter-cultural misunderstandings.

04.4 The leadership of this organization is sensitive to the work related needs and concerns of culturally diverse employees.

04.4 Organization policies are administered fairly, uniformly and consistently among employees of all cultural backgrounds.

05. Empowerment

05.1 My ideas and suggestions are valued here.

05.2 I am personally encouraged to be creative and innovative here.

05.3 I have reasonable opportunities to try my own ideas on the job.

05.4 I am appropriately involved in making decisions that affect my work.

05.5 Rewards in this organization are appropriately shared among those who deserve them.

06. Growth & Advancement

06.1 There are good opportunities here for me to learn new job skills.

06.2 There are good opportunities here to advance to better job.

06.3 Most of the better jobs here are filled from within the organization.

06.4 Employees here are given fair consideration for advancement.

06.5 I believe that I have a good future with this organization.

07. Health & Safety

07.1 The health and safety conditions in my work unit are good.

07.2 The leadership of this organization promptly responds to safety problems.

07.3 In this organization safety has a very high priority.

07.4   There is a continuous program of safety education and training here.

07.5   The employees in my work group have a high degree of safety awareness.

08.   Job Performance

08.1   I understand what the performance standards are for my job.

08.2   I receive regular feedback about how well I am performing my job.

08.3   I receive all of the resources and support that I need to do my job properly.

08.4   I am usually given recognition when I do a good job.

08.5   I feel motivated to fully meet or exceed the performance goals for my job.

09.   Organization Practices

09.1   I believe that the business of this organization is conducted effectively.

09.2   In general, we have a very productive work force here.

09.3   The leadership here responds to the needs and concerns of all employees.

09.4   Most of the leaders in this organization are effective in their individual jobs.

09.5   I get all of the information that I need about the business of this organization.

10.   Performance Commitment

10.1   The leadership of this organization is committed to achieving total quality performance.

10.2   We are all committed to continuously improve the performance of our organization.

10.3   We continuously look for better ways to do things in my work group.

10.4   The leadership of this organization acts decisively to correct any quality or performance problems that might arise.

10.5   The employees in my work group consistently try to meet or exceed job quality standards.

11. Policies & Procedures

11.1 I understand the general policies and work rules of this organization.

11.2 The policies and work rules of this organization make sense.

11.3 Organization policies and work rules are administered fairly here.

11.4 I understand what the specific work procedures are for my job.

11.5 The work procedures for my job are accurate and current.

12. Product & Service Quality

12.1 Quality standards have been established for all of our products and services.

12.2 Our finished products and services fully meet our customers' requirements.

12.3 Our products and services have an excellent reputation for quality.

12.4 Quality is designed and built into all of our products and services.

12.5 Statistical methods are used to ensure the quality of our products and services.

13. Reaction to Survey

13.1 I am comfortable with the confidentiality of this survey.

13.2 This survey has been a good way for me to candidly express my opinions.

13.3 The issues in this survey are important to me.

13.4 This survey demonstrates that my opinions are important to this organization.

13.5 I believe that the results of this survey will be used constructively.

14. Supervisory Leadership

14.1 My supervisor/team leader is willing to listen to my problems or complaints.

14.2 My supervisor/team leader is an effective coach and trainer.

14.3 My supervisor /team leader is an effective problem solver.

14.4   My supervisor/team leader treats all employees fairly and uniformly.

14.5   My supervisor/team leader sets a good example for me to follow.

15.   Teamwork & Cooperation

15.1   There is a lot of teamwork between organization leadership and the employees.

15.2   Members of organization leadership work together effectively as a team.

15.3   There is a lot of teamwork among the employees in my work group.

15.4   My supervisor/team leader encourages teamwork within my work group.

1.5   There is a lot of teamwork between the different work groups here.

16.   The Job Itself

16.1   My job is interesting.

16.2   My job makes good use of my skills and abilities.

16.3   I usually feel a sense of accomplishment when I complete my job.

16.4   I feel that my job is important to the success of this organization.

16.5   I enjoy the duties and responsibilities of my job.

17.   Training and Education

17.1   I have received the training that I need to do my job properly.

17.2   New employees are given effective initial job training.

17.3   Employees receive continuous education and training to develop their job skills.

17.4   My work group has received training in ways to improve its team effectiveness.

17.5   Employees are properly trained about the business and products of this organization.

18.   Values and Ethics

18.1   I understand this organization=s code of values and ethics.
18.2   The leadership of this organization conducts business in an ethical manner.
18.3   I am proud of the social consciousness of the leadership of this organization.
18.4   The leadership of this organization consistently fulfills its community responsibility.
18.5   The employees in my work group conduct themselves in accordance with the organization=s code of values and ethics.

19.   Work Conditions

19.1   The general physical conditions in my work area are good.
19.2   The heating and ventilation in my work area are good.
19.3   My work area is free from unpleasant odors and fumes.
19.4   My work area is free from excessive noise and distraction.
19.5   There is good lighting in my work area.

20.   Work Group Performance

20.1   I understand the performance standards that have been established for my work group.
20.2   My work group consistently meets or exceeds its quality goals.
20.3   My work group has a low level of scrap, waste and rework.
20.4   My work group consistently meets or exceeds its production goals.
20.5   The main focus in my work group is on high quality work performance.

Appendix D
Sample Survey Report
& Scoring Guidelines

The Talico survey report presents survey findings in narrative, tabular and graphic form. All sections of the report have been designed so that the information and data can be easily understood by most management level employees. This section of the manual will discuss the survey report format and explain how you can interpret the information and data that your survey report contains in a meaningful way.

The report begins with a narrative section or Executive Overview that presents a quick snapshot of major survey findings. That section contains information about the number of employees who participated in the survey, the general level of satisfaction that employees seem to have with organizational conditions measured by the survey and a list of survey issues that were rated by employees as being either most positive or least positive. The Executive Overview also includes two tabular and graphic presentations of the survey data for the organization as a whole, a summary of survey scores for the twelve survey categories that were measured (each category representing a composite score for the four individual survey items comprising the category) and an All Respondents report that shows individual survey item scores.

Figure D-1, Summary of Survey Categories Report, presents composite scores for a selection of survey categories or sets. Statistical data in Figure D-1 are presented both in terms of arithmetic means and as a distribution of response percentages. The latter scores fall in three groups: Strengths (Str), Neutral (Neu) and Weaknesses (Wkn). A colorful "fever chart" (reproduced in this manual in gray scale) helps the reader quickly spot areas of particular strengths or weaknesses. Figure D-2, All Respondents Report, contains the same type of information but for individual survey items rather than for survey category composites. Because the data and information for individual survey items is diagnostically more useful than that for survey categories this discussion will focus on the former.

You will recall that the Talico EOS consists of sets of individual survey items. These sets are called categories or measurement dimensions. Each set of items is interrelated and have been selected because together they cover the domain of a particular measurement subject, like communication. The **Communication** survey category, therefore, is comprised of a set of individual items that measure various benchmark attributes of organizational communication. Referring again to Figure D-2, you will observe that the **Communication** category consists of the following four individual survey items:

1.   Communication from management is open and honest.

2.   Employees are free to speak up and say what they think.

3.   I get all of the information that I need to do my job properly.

4.   My supervisor is an accurate, reliable source of information.

(Note: the items in the sample Communication set are taken from the standard, vs. customized, EOS. Thus, they have only four items per set compared with five items as in most customized surveys.)

There is an important reason why those particular four items were chosen to represent the domain of communication. They represent the four most important attributes of organizational communication: credibility of management communication, freedom to speak up without fear of reprisal, job-related information sufficiency, and the immediate supervisor as the primary source of accurate, timely and sufficient job related information. Further, there is a self-validating component in this set. For example, studies have found that it is unlikely that employees will feel free to speak up candidly under conditions when they believe that communication from management is not frank and honest. Thus, a high score in one of those two items with a low score in the other suggests that some kind of anomaly might exist in the response pattern and that further investigation may be advisable.

Figure D-2 shows individual item scores for three categories, Communication, Management Practices and Teamwork & Cooperation. In the Talico EOS we have designated that "high score" is best with "Strongly Agree" having a value of

5 and "Strongly Disagree" having a value of 1. "Strengths" are essentially percentages of positive response. In the Composite survey 59.2% of the employees agreed with or responded positively to the statement that "Communication from management is frank and honest." The same line item shows that 21.5% of the employees were undecided about the credibility of management communication while 19.3% were negative.

So, how are you to decide whether a survey score is satisfactory or not? One way is for your organization's management to set its own standard and measure survey performance against that yardstick. However, we can offer our experience in this matter. Over the years we have experientially concluded that "good" scores begin at about 70% positive response (Str). From 60% through 69% positive scores are marginal to somewhat positive and scores that fall below 60% usually signal likely problem issues. In the sample All Respondents Report, for example, 54.1% of employees were positive about the credibility of management communication and 23.2% were negative about it. Twenty-two point seven percent seem to be uncertain? It is obvious that the nature of this particular survey item is such that any management would want as high a score as possible. By combining the undecided or neutral scores you can see that 45.9% of the employees feel less than positive about the credibility of management communication. Further, the 54.1% positive score is less than the experiential 60% threshold indicating either a possible problem issue or at best a marginal issue.

A quick glance at Figure D-2 will show you the value of the Talico EOS report format. The "fever chart" shows that 85.2% of employees opined that "There is a lot of teamwork among the employees in my work group." However, only 49.2% of the respondents seem to believe that "There is a lot of teamwork between management and the employees." Obviously the latter is an issue that will be of concern to management while the former is an important organizational strength. The graphic presentation of data in the report helps the reader to quickly make comparisons between strengths and weaknesses like these two issues.

The information that can be obtained from studying survey data has many potential uses. In the above sample it can be seen that management would want to reassess their communication practices to learn why some employees question management communication credibility and related issues. They would want to learn why employees perceive that there is not sufficient teamwork among the management team itself. But, they would also want to build on the positives or near positives like management's success in developing a productive work force and the perceived effectiveness of individual managers and supervisors. Further, only a sample of the All Respondents Report is shown in Figure D-2. The full survey report contains many other items that relate to employee skill development and which can be used by HRD and training professionals to develop programs to boost job skills. Most Talico surveys also provide a write-in comment section where employees can offer suggestions for organization improvement, like ways to cut costs or increase operating efficiencies or to express concerns not addressed in the structured part of the survey questionnaire. In these cases the Talico survey report also contains an optional verbatim transcript of comments.

Another way to evaluate the significance of survey data is to compare the organization's scores to normative data. All Talico survey reports are accompanied by a set of norms for each survey item that is in the Talico survey item data bank (usually included as part of the Executive Overview section of the report). These norms have been collected and regularly updated over a 25 year period. While the norms can serve as an evaluation guide there seems to be a considerable misunderstanding among many executives and managers about their value and utility.

The purpose of a norm, with respect to the reporting of survey data, is to provide a benchmark against which an organization can compare its own survey scores. But, management must understand that a norm is only a weighted average – not necessarily a goal to achieve. Suppose that the norm for a survey item measuring the confidence that employees have in senior management's leadership ability is 55% positive response. That means that on the average 55% of all employees who have responded to that item in the Talico data base have a positive perception about the leadership ability of their senior management. But by the same measure, it means that 45% either are not confident about the leadership ability of their senior management or they cannot be sure about it – a very disturbing situation. The management of an organization that surveys its employees and scores, say, 50% positive response for that item should hardly set 55%, the norm in this case, as its goal for improvement. Even when it achieves 55% there is still a very long way to go before it could claim that its employees are confident in its senior management's leadership ability.

The Talico EOS report to management is an important diagnostic tool. Because of the convenient report format management can quickly spot issues the indicate organizational strengths or weaknesses. By comparing the All Respondents survey data with data for each survey subgroup management can identify internal anomalies and variances from the internal norm. Management can also use the normative data supplied by Talico to obtain a sense of how the scores for their organization compare with those of other organizations. In all cases the information and data that the survey report provides management can be used as an objective and meaningful decision base upon which organizational improvement programs can be constructed.

Figure D-1 Summary of Survey Categories Report

Questions	Mean	0 20 40 60 80100	Wkn%	Neu%	Str%
Communication	3.78		12.7	14.1	73.3
Diversity	3.60		9.0	31.8	59.2
Empowerment	3.23		26.1	23.9	50.0
Education/Training	3.03		32.8	27.1	40.1
Job Performance	3.74		14.6	14.8	70.6
Management Practices	3.45		14.4	30.0	55.6
Policies & Goals	3.80		9.4	15.3	75.3
Product/Service Quality	3.95		6.3	15.5	78.2
Supervisory Leadership	3.97		8.4	13.6	77.9
Teamwork & Cooperation	3.60		15.3	23.5	61.1
The Job Itself	3.62		15.9	18.9	65.2
Work Conditions	3.84		11.9	14.0	74.1
Grand Mean	3.63		14.7	20.2	65.1

Weaknesses (Wkn)   Neutral (Neu)   Strengths (Str)

Figure D-2 All Respondents Report

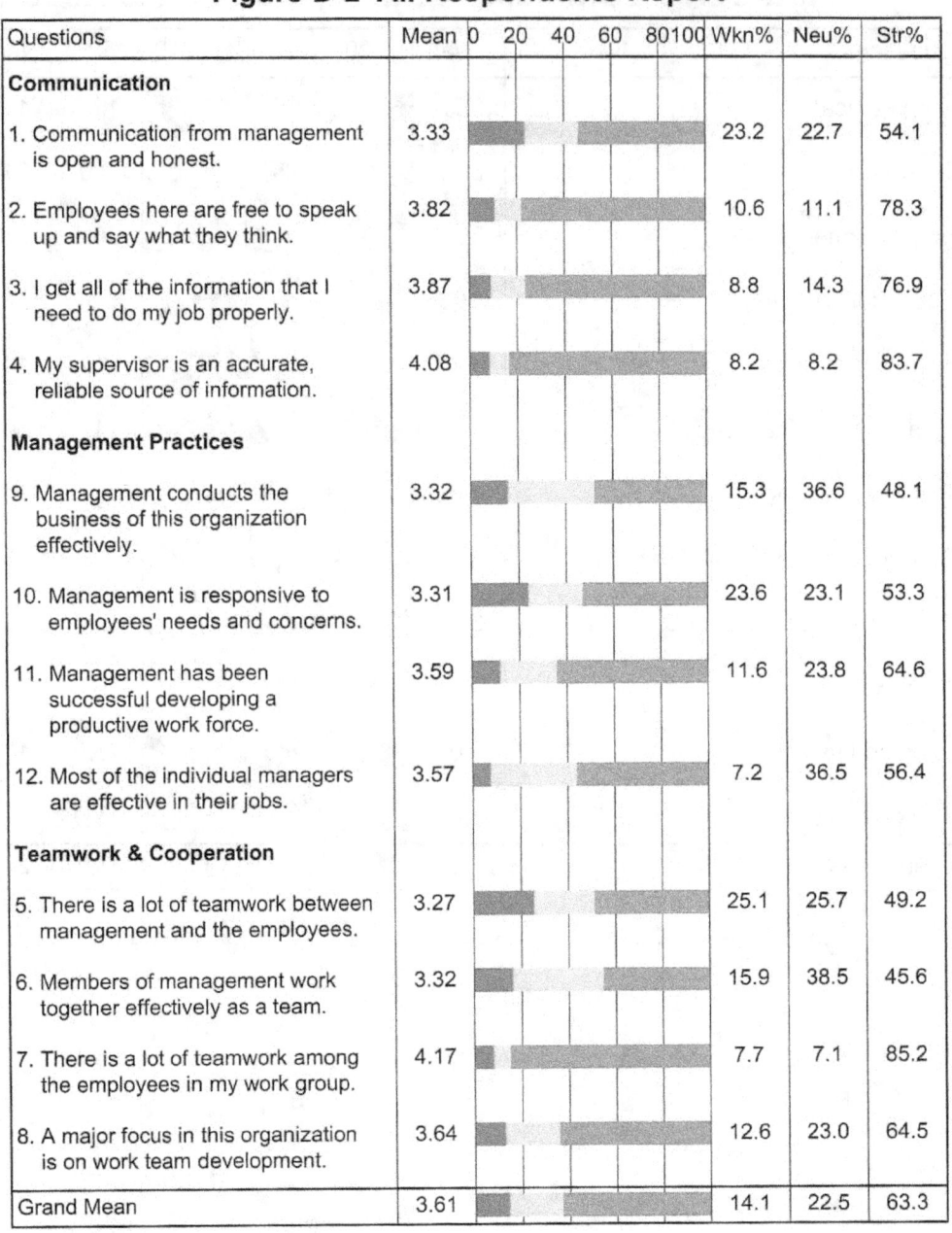

Questions	Mean	0 20 40 60 80 100	Wkn%	Neu%	Str%
Communication					
1. Communication from management is open and honest.	3.33		23.2	22.7	54.1
2. Employees here are free to speak up and say what they think.	3.82		10.6	11.1	78.3
3. I get all of the information that I need to do my job properly.	3.87		8.8	14.3	76.9
4. My supervisor is an accurate, reliable source of information.	4.08		8.2	8.2	83.7
Management Practices					
9. Management conducts the business of this organization effectively.	3.32		15.3	36.6	48.1
10. Management is responsive to employees' needs and concerns.	3.31		23.6	23.1	53.3
11. Management has been successful developing a productive work force.	3.59		11.6	23.8	64.6
12. Most of the individual managers are effective in their jobs.	3.57		7.2	36.5	56.4
Teamwork & Cooperation					
5. There is a lot of teamwork between management and the employees.	3.27		25.1	25.7	49.2
6. Members of management work together effectively as a team.	3.32		15.9	38.5	45.6
7. There is a lot of teamwork among the employees in my work group.	4.17		7.7	7.1	85.2
8. A major focus in this organization is on work team development.	3.64		12.6	23.0	64.5
Grand Mean	3.61		14.1	22.5	63.3

▓ Weaknesses (Wkn)   ░ Neutral (Neu)   ▒ Strengths (Str)

**Appendix E
Action Planning Supplement**

Action Planning Supplement

There are actually two parts to the process of survey-guided action planning. The first phase begins with senior management's review of the survey results that occurs during the **Reporting and Feedback** phase of the survey project plan. Included in that phase are two management reviews. The purpose of the first management review is principally to familiarize senior management with the survey results and to obtain a general "sensing" of their reaction to the data. Then, after a short incubation period, all or a specifically appointed team of senior management reconvenes for a working session. It is this latter session that begins the action planning process as we are defining it.

- A general overview of what should occur during the second management review was provided earlier in this manual. Below is a more detailed outline of the specific tasks that the management team should be performing at that time:

- The team conducts a general discussion about the survey findings. Individual team members express their personal feelings about the data and share any general concerns that they might have about survey issues.

- The team then begins to analyze the survey data. Key issues that may have an adverse effect on organizational performance are identified. The issues are separated into two groups. The first of these are *systemic* issues.

- Systemic issues or problems are those that are common to the organization as a whole. They affect many people for long periods of time and they can affect people at various organizational levels. Thus, systemic problems are basically of the same form for many people throughout the organization. A perception that getting the product or service produced or provided is more important that quality or safety would be an example of a systemic problem. Systemic problems can also occur when a problem is found only among one or a very few organizational groups but when the

66

functioning of those groups is crucial the overall success of the organization.

- Another class of problems is *local* in nature and scope. This type of problem is not common throughout the organization, nor does it usually cross hierarchical lines. An illustration of a local or departmental problem would be the case when a significant number of employees in a particular work group (but not necessarily in other work groups) believe that their supervisor is not giving them proper job skills training.

- The team then focuses on systemic problems. Criteria used for prioritization usually include both the beneficial effect that solving the problem will have on organization performance and the extent to which the problem is controllable. For example, an environmental problem may be subject to complex and extensive state or federal laws which may place its resolution beyond the limits of authority of organizational management. At its discretion management may also choose to add other prioritization criteria unique to their particular operations or circumstances.

- After prioritizing issues the team then looks for close similarities and clear redundancies. These are combined or eliminated as appropriate.

- Next, a brief description is written for the top three to five priority issues. This is done to ensure common understanding among the team and to better identify the full nature of the issues that will now become the center of problem solving activities. This is a very important step. Unless everyone is clear about the specific problem issues considerable time and effort can be wasted in an attempt to solve the wrong problem!

- Using cause-effect analysis or other methods, the team determines the root cause of each priority problem. They then develop a set of alternative strategies to deal with each problem, evaluate the merits of the alternatives and select the alternative or alternatives that in their judgement will most effectively resolve the problem issue. Responsibilities for dealing with the various problems are assigned and appropriate control measures are established.

- Local or departmental problems are assigned to subordinate level managers who have responsibility for the areas in which the problems have been found. They, in turn, convene problem solving meetings with their subordinates and follow the same basic process as described above to deal with those issues. However, they also have the responsibility to report back to senior management after an agreed period of time for both status and results reporting purposes.

Obviously, the actual problem solving process that you will use to deal with any problems identified in your survey will be more extensive than that briefly outlined above. Most problem solving activities of this type require several weeks to complete and they often involve employees from several different work units or functions. In fact, an important part of the problem solving inclusion process can involve large groups of employees who provide additional information about problem issues as well as suggestions for change and improvement. The core of this process of inclusion is information gathered during focus group meetings or interviews, the next subject of this section.

Focus Group Meetings

First, we suggest that you review items number 26-31 in the Survey Planning Guide of this manual. All of those items are relevant to the subject of focus group meetings or interviews and will refresh your recollection about the purpose, intent and methodology of arranging for and conducting focus group meetings. In this section of the appendix you will be familiarized with the methods and techniques of focus group interviewing. The information that is contained in this section will be a valuable aid to those who are appointed as facilitators of focus group meetings.

Group Size & Composition

It is worth reemphasizing that you should make every effort to restrict the size of the focus group to no more than eight to ten employees if possible. Larger size groups greatly tend to inhibit free flowing discussion and groups that are smaller than eight, especially when they fall below six, can too easily be influenced by only one or two "vocal" employees. Also, be sure that the manager or supervisor of the employees comprising the focus group is not included in the same meeting group. The presence of the "boss" also can produce an adverse effect on the openness of discussion during the meeting. It is possible, for example, that the problem employees are having is caused by or at least influenced by their immediate supervisor. They will be more likely to discuss that issue openly if the supervisor is not present in the meeting.

Taking Notes

The purpose of the meetings is to produce information. If this information is not transmitted during the discussion then the meeting was of no value. The information link is the meeting facilitator, who must ensure that notes of the discussion are taken. No one can be expected of retaining all of the information that is discussed during a focus group meeting in his or her head without the benefit of note. Further, most meeting participants will expect that the facilitator, or someone else in the session, will be taking notes. On the other hand, note taking can have a negative affect on the discussion if done poorly. Note taking should be done unobtrusively but openly. Meeting participants must be assured that although the essence of what they say may be noted, their comments will not be associated with them personally in any way.

Because of this we recommend that the facilitator ask for one or more volunteers from the group to serve as note takers. This usually adds a degree of comfort to the meeting and at the same time frees the facilitator so that he or she can concentrate on developing information. Notes can be made on standard note pads, on a lap top word processor or even on a flip chart. The facilitator should give general guidelines about what should and should not be recorded and can ask the note taker to be sure that certain points are recorded after they are made. One important guideline is that note takers should wait until a person has finished speaking before making a note. This is both courteous to the speaker and also avoids the pitfall of unconsciously signaling the speaker as to the importance of the point that he or she is making.

After the meeting is over the notes should be made available for review by the meeting participants. This reinforces that anonymity of individual response was honored and it also gives meeting participants the chance to ensure the accuracy of the notes. When the review of the notes is finished the facilitator should take responsibility for them and should have them transcribed for later use and distribution.

Interview Style

Most professional facilitators have their own personal style for conducting focus group meetings. Some are more formal than others. What is most important is for the facilitator to be seen as behaving in a friendly, open and trustful way. This writer's own preference is to dispense with jokes or irrelevant comments about the weather or sports and instead proceed to thank participant for their willingness to attend the meeting and then review the meeting's purpose, objectives and ground rules. A short statement about the anonymity of individual comments and a brief explanation about how the meeting results will be used then leads directly into the discussion. In other words, the facilitator should be friendly and somewhat relaxed but also businesslike and always professional. The focus group meeting will last only an hour or at most an hour and one-half and the facilitator must ensure that the meeting objectives are accomplished in that time frame. There is not much time for the irrelevant. Besides, most people respect facilitators who are also good meeting leaders. People want meaningful, well-run meetings.

One last note dealing with interview style, always end the meeting on a positive note. State that you believe the meeting was very constructive and helpful. Thanks the participants again for their involvement and let them know that they will be kept informed about further management response actions and decisions to the survey and to the focus group meeting information.

Interviewing Techniques

It is crucial that the facilitator refrain from interjecting his or her own feelings about survey issues into the meeting discussion. Failure to follow this key rule is the primary cause of focus group meeting failure. This is a very difficult rule to follow for many senior executives and for their line management subordinates, especially if they feel personally threatened by survey results. For example, in one case a senior executive held a series of post-survey focus group meetings with a cross-section of the employees in his area of responsibility. Instead of using the meetings to gain a better understanding about the priority issues of concern to the employees and about their suggestions for improvement, the executive spent most of the time expressing his disappointment that the survey scores were low. You can imagine the effect that this had on the quality and value of the meetings.

In other cases line managers who chose to conduct the focus group meetings themselves have spent half the period justifying organization policy and trying to persuade employees that their perceptions were incorrect. This type of behavior is not only certain to doom the value of the focus group meeting but also of the entire survey itself. It is mainly because of this that we recommend that focus group facilitation be handled by a person experienced in group process techniques.

One of the most important facilitation techniques that should be used is the questioning technique. There are two types of questions, *direct* and *indirect*. Although almost inevitably necessary at one time or another, direct questions offer the possibility, if not likelihood, of a "yes" or "no" answer. Indirect questions, on the other hand, do not lend themselves to "yes" or "no" answers but rather are sufficiently open-ended that they usually elicit important new information.

For example, suppose that a facilitator wants to learn about the satisfaction that an employee has with her job. The facilitator could ask a direct question such as "Are you satisfied with your job?" But, instead of eliciting any meaningful details about the employee's job satisfaction, the question could simply elicit a "Yes, I am" response. But, consider the greater opportunity to obtain information about the employee's degree of job satisfaction that would occur if the facilitator phrased the question this way: "I am very interested in learning how you feel about your job. Please tell me some of the things that you find most satisfying and also some of the things that you like least about it." There is no possibility of a "yes" or "no" answer here.

Once the employee begins to respond to a question the facilitator must keep the ball rolling. Here are a few ways that this can be done:

- Show understanding and acceptance with a nod of the head or by saying something neutral like "I see."

- Remain silent but nod your head or use a facial expression in a way that implies you want to hear more.

- Restate the speaker's main thought but do not add anything to it. For example, "You feel that the company does not allow enough sick days."

- State what you understand the speaker to have said but do not add anything to it. For example, "If I understand what you just said correctly, you believe that management is not sincere about wanting to learn how employees really feel about work conditions here."

Periodically during the meeting the facilitator should summarize the main points discussed to ensure that the facilitator clearly understands the participants' perceptions and to reassure participants that he or she does understand them.

During the meeting the facilitator must ensure that all group members participate in the discussion. Failure to do this can easily skew the results to favor the comments of only those participants who are the most vocal. One way to ensure full participation is to ask each person in turn how he or she feels about a certain point or issue. But a more relaxed, though equally effective, way is to ask an employee the extent that he or she agrees with what one of the speakers has just said. For example, "Mary, how do you feel about what James just described?" The facilitator can use this technique at random during the discussion ensuring that at one time or another there is total inclusion. It should be obvious that indirect questioning will produce the best results when this technique is used.

Processing Focus Group Meeting Information

After all of the focus group meetings are completed the facilitator must consolidate all of the comments from the many notes that were taken. This is a big job. In most cases the notes should first be typed to make reading them easier. The facilitator should then take the typed notes and content analyze them. The easiest way to do this is to look for key words or terms and list them by type and frequency. In other words, the facilitator should look for patterns like expressed concerns about fair treatment, the sufficiency of job skills training, the unavailability of tools or equipment, communication sufficiency, accuracy and timeliness and similar issues. Like issues should be grouped together, refined, clearly defined and verbatim excerpts from the notes should be used to further clarify problems, concerns and suggestions for improvement.

The next step is for the facilitator to prepare a report of focus group meeting findings and to present it to the senior management team. That team then has the task of relating information from the focus group meetings to the data from the statistical and write-in comments parts of the survey. In most cases they will find that the focus group meeting information confirms or validates the earlier survey data but that it provides much greater depth with respect to understanding the basis for employees' concerns.

Appendix F
Sample Survey Questionnaire

Employee Opinion Survey

Your opinions about your job, management and supervisory practices, work conditions and other job-related matters are important to the success of this organization. We invite you to participate in this survey and to candidly express your opinions about these issues. Please complete the section below which is for statistical purposes only. Then turn to the reverse side of this form and follow the instructions for competing the survey. Your responses are confidential and will not identify you personally in any way.

My Job Status Is:

❏ 1. Management/Supervision
❏ 2. Professional/Technical
❏ 3. Office/Clerical
❏ 4. Other

My Work Group Is:

❏ 1. Group A
❏ 2. Group B
❏ 3. Group C
❏ 4. Group C

When you have completed this survey please return the form to the survey facilitator in your organization. Thank you.

Version EOS.2

Instructions

Read each of the following survey items carefully. Decide on the extent to which you agree or disagree with each of the statements and then place a mark (**X**) in the column to the right of each statement that most accurately expresses your opinion. Make suggestions or comments in the **Comments** section.

Survey Items	Strongly Disagree	Disagree	Uncertain	Agree	Strongly Agree
1. Communication from management is open and honest.	1	2	3	4	5
2. Employees here are free to speak up and say what they think.	1	2	3	4	5
3 . I get all of the information I need to do my job properly.	1	2	3	4	5
4. I understand the performance standards for my job.	1	2	3	4	5
5. I understand how well I am performing my job.	1	2	3	4	5
6. I am motivated to meet or exceed the performance standards of my job.	1	2	3	4	5
7. We are all committed to meet our customers' needs and expectations.	1	2	3	4	5
8. Our products/services have an excellent reputation for quality.	1	2	3	4	5
9. Our finished products/services fully satisfy our customers.	1	2	3	4	5
10. The health and safety conditions in my work unit are good.	1	2	3	4	5
11. In this organization safety has a very high priority.	1	2	3	4	5
12. In general the work conditions in my area are good.	1	2	3	4	5
13. My supervisor treats all employees fairly and uniformly.	1	2	3	4	5
14. My supervisor is willing to listen to my problems or complaints.	1	2	3	4	5
15. My supervisor is an effective coach and trainer.	1	2	3	4	5
16. There is a lot of teamwork among the employees in my work group.	1	2	3	4	5
17. There is a lot of teamwork among the different work groups here.	1	2	3	4	5
18. There is a lot of teamwork between management and employees.	1	2	3	4	5
19. I have received the training that I need to do my job properly.	1	2	3	4	5
20. My job makes good use of my skills and abilities.	1	2	3	4	5
21. I receive recognition when I do good work.	1	2	3	4	5
22. Overall, I like my job.	1	2	3	4	5
23. Overall, management in this organization does a good job.	1	2	3	4	5
24. Overall, this is a good place to work.	1	2	3	4	5

Comments:

_____

_____

_____

_____

_____

Notes

Notes